Before You Go To Bed

By the same author

BEFORE YOU GROW UP
DODIE

Finola Akister

Illustrated by Colin West

VIKING KESTREL

VIKING KESTREL
Published by the Penguin Group
27 Wrights Lane, London W8 5TZ, England
Viking Penguin Inc., 40 West 23rd Street, New York, New York 10010, USA
Penguin Books Australia Ltd, Ringwood, Victoria, Australia
Penguin Books Canada Ltd, 2801 John Street, Markham, Ontario, Canada L3R 1B4
Penguin Books (NZ) Ltd, 182–190 Wairau Road, Auckland 10, New Zealand

Penguin Books Ltd, Registered Offices: Harmondsworth, Middlesex, England

First published 1989
1 3 5 7 9 10 8 6 4 2

Filmset in Century Schoolbook (Linotron 202) by
Rowland Phototypesetting (London) Ltd

Printed in Great Britain by Butler and Tanner Ltd, Frome, Somerset

A CIP catalogue record for this book is available from the British Library

ISBN 0–670–82329–5

I woke up in the morning
Feeling kind of 'off'.
Will I develop lots of spots
Or just a nasty cough?
But then my best friend called to see
If I'd go out to play.
Suddenly I felt ever so well –
One does on Saturday.

'I have a very sore throat,' said Jemima,
'And I'm in so much terrible pain,
My voice has gone scratchy and squeaky,
Will I ever get better again?'
'It will take a long time,' said her doctor,
'It's a thing at which no one should laugh,
It's the worst sort of germ you could possibly have,
As you happen to be a giraffe.'

I had a little tadpole,
I found it in a bog.
Some legs it grew and then I knew
I had a little frog.

Where can I locate an ant-eater?
I've never seen one about town.
And the ants' nests that litter my garden
Are undoubtedly getting me down.

If you happen to see such a creature
Will you stop him, and just to please me,
Invite him to dine, he can come any time,
For breakfast or dinner or tea.

Mary, Mary, quite contrary,
How does your garden fare?
'Well the plants grow I guess,
But I have to confess,
I've got thousands of weeds everywhere.'

11

There's a very, very pretty rose
In the hedge for all to see.
They've told me it's a wild rose,
But it looks quite tame to me.

Roses are red
Violets are blue
I don't really think that's right,
Do you?
Some roses are red
I guess that's true,
But violets are violet –
BLUEBELLS are blue.

Chomp, chomp, went the caterpillar
Till he'd eaten all the leaf.
Then because there was nothing to cling to
He fell to the ground underneath.

14

If you have a nice voice and you sing like a lark,
Or some other bird you might hear in the park,
You can break into song at the drop of a hat
But, not if you happen to sing like a cat.
A cat sings his songs in the dead of the night.
It is not like the music Beethoven would write.
It's a horrible noise, now I come to recall,
It's not really like any music at all.

Mary had a little lamb
Its fleece she went and sold.
Now she has a woolly jumper,
But the lamb is feeling cold.

The other day I chanced to see
A pussy-cat who winked at me.
I said, 'Hello, I hope you're well,'
But what he answered I couldn't tell.
He said 'Meow', but you can see
It didn't mean a thing to me.
I asked him, in a friendly way,
How many mice he'd caught that day.
But again he only said 'Meow'
Which didn't mean a lot somehow.
To show how friendly I could be
I asked him would he come to tea.
'Meow' was all he said, and then
I noticed that he winked again.
I could not understand this cat.
In school they taught me this and that,
But not what one should do or say
To a cat one meets upon the way.
I wasn't getting anywhere
So I said 'Goodbye' and left him there.

Ding-dong bell
Puss is in the well.
She jumped in by the merest whim
And then found out she could not swim.

My mother was a blackbird,
She lived up in a tree.
She laid an egg,
She kept it warm,
It hatched
And there was
Me.

There's a special chair in our house,
It's Daddy's chair.
There's another one just like it,
And my mum sits there.
There's a special chair for Grandad,
Then the one for Gran makes four,
I haven't got a special chair
So I sit on the floor.

Mirror high upon the wall,
What use are you to me?
You're fine for people who are tall,
But I'm only three foot three.

I picked up a pencil to draw
A picture to hang on the wall.
A portrait of Dad, but it really was bad,
It didn't look like him at all.
Then Dad said that he'd draw a picture of me –
He picked up the pencil and tried,
It was such a mess that I have to confess
That we laughed and we laughed till we cried.

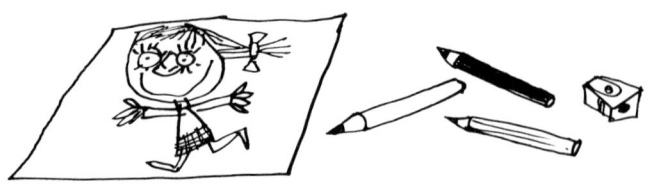

I was playing with my train set
One rainy afternoon,
When all at once I saw a mouse
Was running round the room.
I didn't quite know what to do,
I thought of this and that,
Then the mouse ran up to me and said,
'Please save me from the cat.'
So I hid the little fellow,
He had such appealing eyes.
And Puss Cat never knew
That I had robbed him of his prize.
I gave the cat some extra food
To try and make amends,
But I dare not ever tell him
That the mouse and I are friends.

The pitter-patter of tiny feet
Ran quickly across the floor,
They pitted and they patted
Till they reached the pantry door.
I'd been asleep before the fire –
It was comfy and warm on the mat.
I didn't bother to chase that mouse,
Because I'm a lazy cat.

I got up in the morning,
Put on my coat and hat,
I trotted off to market
To purchase 'This' and 'That'.
Now 'This' was very easy –
I bought it straight away,
But 'That' was much more difficult –
There was none about that day.
So I went off home without 'That',
It was not what I would wish,
Because I had to eat my chips
Without some lovely fish.

It was an early day in spring
I saw the most amazing thing.
A singing thrush just flying by
Stopped as this strange thing caught his eye.
Then out of curiosity
Flew down to earth and sat by me.
An earthworm popped out of his hole,
Then next to him a furry mole.
A rabbit, much to his surprise,
Said he could not believe his eyes.
A wasp and then a busy bee
Buzzed down to see what they could see.
A fox and lots of angry hounds
Came rushing up in leaps and bounds,

Then quickly stopped and joined the throng
That gazed on this phenomenon.
Horses came and horsemen too
Joined with this mixed and motley crew,
Who stood around and gazed in awe
Upon the strange thing that they saw.
I did not know what it could be –
It was a perfect mystery.
Then with a sort of purring sound
It lifted quickly from the ground.
It flew away at such a pace
And soon was lost in outer space.

If you don't want to go
And you really don't know
How to get there
Or how to come back,
You might as well stay
Where you happen to be,
But perhaps you prefer
To go off on a spree.
If you don't know the way
And you want to explore,
You can ask someone clever
Who's been there before.
If they won't tell you
Don't cry in dismay,
If you look at the map
It will show you the way.

'I'd like to go outside,'
Said Jane one sunny day.
'But first I'll ask my mother
If I can go out to play.
I think my mother will agree
But if it starts to rain,
I won't stay out and get all wet,
I'll come back in again.'

Archibald was full of pluck
But, sad to say, had rotten luck.
He wished to travel wide and far
But lacked the vital stamina.
Still, Archibald would not give in
And one day, by the merest whim,
He put on running shoes and shorts
And entered in the local sports.

He was surprised that he'd signed on
To run a five-mile marathon.
He knew before the race began
That he would be an also-ran,
Still none the less and just the same
Our lad was nothing if not game.
He'd have a go but knew he'd lack
The energy to stagger back.

He started with a gentle trot
Like people do who jog a lot.
The first mile almost crippled him,
His body ached in every limb.
But as the lad was full of pluck,
And by the oddest stroke of luck,
It chanced he trod with leaden feet
Upon a dog out in the street,

Who took a quick dislike and more
To this boy who'd trodden on his paw.
So quickly getting to his feet
He chased our hero down the street.
Then, even though the effort hurt,
Young Archibald put on a spurt,
No longer did he merely jog –
He knew he must outrun the dog.
He hurried at so fast a pace
He actually won the race.

Then with the minimum of fuss
Our Archibald went home by bus.

I had a trip upon a ship.
A ride upon a train.
I'll have to do it in reverse
When I go home again.

Luton is an airport.
For aeroplanes no doubt.
They fly them in,
They turn them round,
And then they fly them out.

They fly to other aerodromes
Away across the sea,
They fly them out,
They turn them round,
And then fly back, you see.

'Come fly with me, come fly with me,'
Said the pilot to the crew.
As they were all inside the aeroplane,
There was nothing much else they could do.

London Bridge was taken down,
It's sad, but let me say,
They built it up and it's just like new
In the good old USA.

There's a monster, they think, up in Scotland
That is swimming around in Loch Ness.
And though some people say they have seen it,
There are those who are doubtful, I guess.

But if there's a monster in Scotland
And it's happily swimming about,
There's no cause for alarm, it is doing no harm
If it stays there and doesn't come out.

He would have liked to gallop
For he had to travel far,
But his horse was old and short of breath –
How he wished he had a car!
The day was drawing to a close,
The light was getting dim.
The old horse stumbled, almost fell
And he feared the horse was ill.
Then he knew that he might never
Reach the town at all.
For he was a knight in armour,
And he knew that each (k)night must fall.

39

'Pardon me, Sir, when I tell you,
There is something I have to relate.
I went for a walk and lingered to talk
To a horse that I met near a gate.
Try to believe when I tell you
This horse was remarkably kind.
In a roundabout way, he warned me to stay
Far away from a thing he had found.
"There is something quite strange in my meadow,
I do not know what it can be,"
Said the horse in a most distressed manner,
"But you're welcome to come in and see.
It looks like a large shiny saucer,"
Said the horse who was showing some fear,
"There's a tiny wee man who keeps bobbing about,
I wish it would all disappear.
What on earth do you think it can be?"
Asked the horse in his kindliest way.
"I fear I don't know," I replied, "Shall we go?
I'm really not eager to stay."
So we left by the gate to the meadow,
And that, Sir, is why you can see
A horse standing here in the classroom,
I brought him along, Sir, with me.
So, pardon me, Sir, when I ask you
To be kind to this horse, for you know,
Until someone gets rid of that thing in his field
This poor horse has nowhere to go.'

If you're going to the moon, you must
Expect to see a lot of dust.
Even worse than that I fear,
There isn't any air up there.
I tell you this for what it's worth,
But I will stay down here on earth.

42

If walking down a busy road
You chance to meet a big fat toad,
Don't call him 'ugly' on the spot,
You'll hurt his feelings quite a lot.
Just warn him not to linger there –
A car might come from anywhere
And run him down and squash him flat.
The toad, you know, would not like that.

'Do you think,' said the tortoise, 'it would matter a lot
    If I walked a bit faster? You know,
There are so many places I'm longing to see
And my progress is painfully slow.'
'I think you're supposed to go slow,' said the hare.
'You have legs that are stubby and short,
And that big heavy shell that you carry about
Shows you're really not fashioned for sport.'
The tortoise looked down at his short stubby legs,
It was true, he was built to go slow,
So hard as it seems he abandoned his dreams
Of the places he wanted to go.

'**D**' is for the Dove of Peace,
It's also for the duck.
There used to be a dodo.
But it died. What rotten luck.

The tiger has stripes all over his coat,
The leopard has spots here and there.
The poor hippopotamus has a proboscis,
The gorilla is covered with hair.
The giraffe has, by heck, a very long neck,
The elephant has a large trunk.
The lion is king of the jungle
But they all run away from the skunk.

Horace was a happy horse
And glad that he was able
To gallop round the fields all day
And sleep all night in the stable.

The yak is a beast that comes from Tibet.
But as I live in England
I haven't seen one yet.

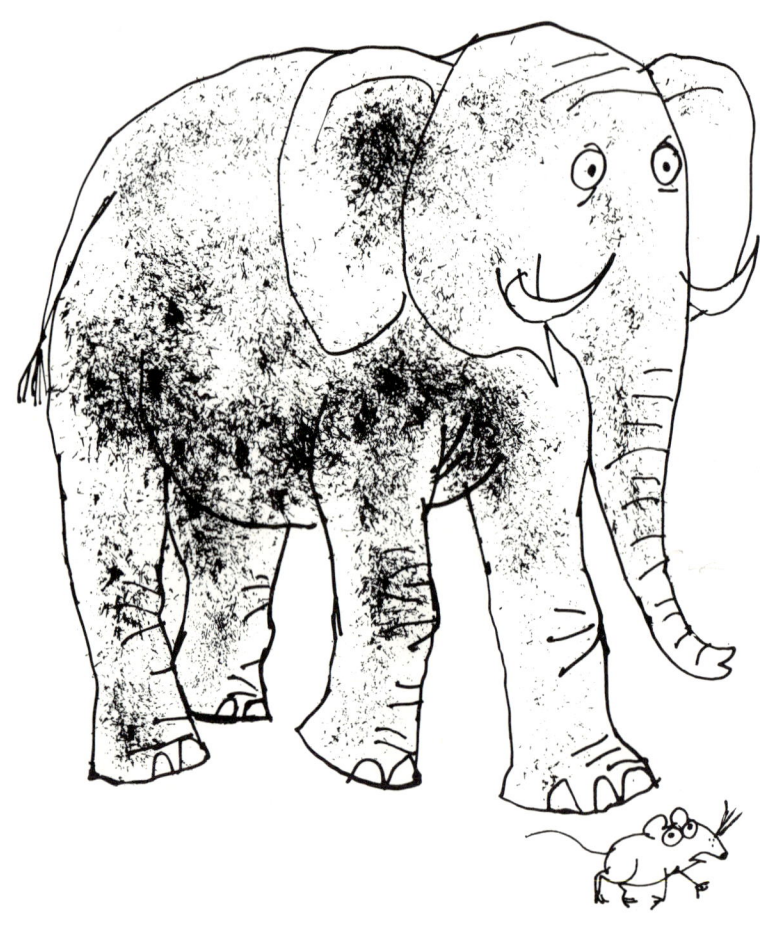

An elephant is big and strong,
Anything he tramples on
Gets squashed.

50

The polar bear, I'd have you know,
Wears a big fur coat, as white as snow.
It is because, you will agree,
It makes him difficult to see
Amongst the snowflakes on the ground.
He isn't very often found.

I beavered away all the morning,
I beavered the whole day through.
When you happen to be a beaver,
There's nothing much else you can do.

Mrs Bear had hibernated
All the winter through.
She went to bed and slept a lot,
There was nothing else to do.
The ground was cold and frozen hard,
The winds were fierce and chill,
So she and little Baby Bear
Slept on and on, until
One morning Mrs Bear woke up
And she said to herself, said she,
'I think the sun is shining,
I'll just pop out and see.'
So Baby Bear and Mrs Bear
Got up and left their den,
Outside the snow was falling fast
So they went back in again.
'I fear, my dear,' said Mrs Bear,
'It's really very plain,
We have woken up too early.'
So they went to sleep again.

Henry was a grasshopper that hopped around a
   lot.
He never walked sedately, he didn't even trot.
This annoyed the creepie-crawlies
Who liked him . . . not a lot.
He leapt in leaps tremendous,
As high as he could leap.
The little creepie-crawlies
Complained they couldn't sleep,
For he made a noise whilst hopping
Like a sort of chirpy cheep.
Now a frog who would a-wooing go
Stopped wooing for a while.
He had noticed Henry hopping
And he smiled an evil smile . . .
His thoughts were of his dinner
And his heart was full of guile.
But Henry saw the hungry frog
And thought it best to flee.

So he took a leap and leapt into
A cup of lemon tea.
The lady who was drinking it
Exclaimed: 'Oh, deary me,

I didn't ask for sugar,
I declined to have some milk,
But an insect in my lemon tea
Is something I can't drink.'
Then she took the cup and Henry
And she tossed them in the sink.
Henry wasn't pleased at all,
He lost his chirpy cheep.
But he made a vow that in future
He would look before he'd leap.

Nobody really loves me.
I'm not pretty or witty or wise.
They say I am dirty and scorn me,
They say I have got beady eyes.
All that they say may be true –
I'm not going to argue with that –
But I wish someone, somewhere, would love me
For I cannot help being a rat.

The octopus has lots of legs
That grow out at all angles.
One day he tried to cross them
And they finished up all tangles.

You might ask me 'Who am I?'
I'm a very special guy
Who is always dressed in style,
I'll have you know.
I'm not a vulgar sort of chap
Who would wear a woolly cap,
It would look odd in all the places that I go.
Oh yes, I'm really very posh,
I wouldn't wear a mackintosh
Not even if it rained the whole day through.
I'm not the common sort of fellow
Who would tote an umbrella,
I'm particular in everything I do.
There's no need to criticize,
You see I'm very highly prized
And I'm worth much more than you would ever
    think.
I have a twinkle in my eye,
I'm a splendid sort of guy,
I'm stupendous, I'm tremendous,
I'm a mink.

The unicorn had one big horn
In the middle of his head.
It's doubtful if he ever lived,
And if he did, he's dead.

My dog is just a little bit of collie,
Plus a small per cent of beagle, it is true.
There's perhaps a touch of Airedale,
Just a hint of lurcher cur,
And no doubt the merest touch of Kerry blue.
He doesn't look at all like any other dog,
With his hair that grows in little kinky tufts.
They admit that he is clever
But they tell me he will never,
No, he'll positively never be allowed to enter
    Cruft's.
But every night when I come home from school
He runs to meet me, wags his tail with glee,
It's the way that he can say
How much he's missed me all the day,
And that's exactly how I want my dog to be.

If you should notice Montague
When walking down the street,
Don't raise your eyebrows in surprise
At his enormous feet.
Of course they'll grow no bigger
And when Montague grows up,
His feet will match the rest of him,
But now he's just a pup.

'I wish,' said Bunny Rabbit,
'I could climb into a tree,
Like my good friend Sammy Squirrel
Who lives quite close to me.
His house is up a tree you know
And he can see all round,
But I can't see as much as him,
'Cause I'm standing on the ground.
Sometimes Sammy asks me
If I'd like to go to tea.
I have to say I'm sorry
But I cannot, don't you see,
I'd like to go to tea with you
But I cannot climb your tree.
You have such sharp and clinging claws
But I have only paddy paws,
And little rabbits, such as me,
Were never meant to climb a tree.'

Some things tend to puzzle me,
Then I want to know,
Why hares can run so very fast,
Why tortoises are slow.
Why all giraffes are tall and thin,
Why the walrus is so fat,
Or why I have to eat my greens?
Are the things I wonder at.

Cornelius made such a fuss
When told to eat his greens.
He didn't like the cabbage,
He refused to eat the beans.
Sometimes he was very rude,
Said cauliflowers were yuk.
He called the carrots Donkey Food
And would not eat them up.

This state of things went on until
Cornelius would go
And turn on the television
To see a cartoon show.

Popeye the sailor-man was on,
He was very strong and tough
'Cause he ate whole tins of spinach
And thought it was jolly good stuff.
From then on Cornelius pondered –
Perhaps he had been very wrong –
So he ate all the green stuff they gave him
And grew up to be big and strong.

'Oh dear,' said the small Bunny Rabbit,
'We always have lettuce for tea,
A dandelion head would be nicer instead,
What a wonderful change it would be.'
'Oh, let us eat lettuce,' said Mother,
'For lettuce is good for a rabbit.
A lettuce a day in the usual way
Becomes you will find, a good habit.'

There was a mouse, a sorry mouse,
He had a mouse-hole in our house.
He had a wife and children four
And a cousin mouse who lived next-door.
One sunny day he wandered out
To see what food lay round about.
He saw some cheese, 'twas in a trap.
He poked his nose in. Silly chap.
Then in a flash, the story goes,
The trap sprang down upon his nose,
It gave him such a heavy clout
It hurt and knocked his teeth right out.
Though he wriggled free, it's understood
It didn't do our mouse much good.
Though our hero isn't dead,
Not a single tooth stayed in his head.
So, should you meet him do not tease,
Don't offer him hard mousetrap cheese
But just the sort that spreads with ease.

Little Jack Horner sat in the corner
Eating a plum-duff pie.
He took out a plum,
Bit a hole in his thumb,
And that's when he started to cry.

I painted a beautiful picture
With some paints that I found on a shelf.
But when I had finished I noticed
I had painted a lot of myself.
My fingers were green and the tip of my nose
Was a mixture of yellow and pink.
My clothes were a mess, but no doubt you can
    guess,
That I washed it all off in the sink.

69

Today I tidied up my toys,
I had to, there's no doubt.
The cupboard door refused to shut
And the toys kept falling out.
So I put them away quite neatly,
I could only just close the door,
But what shall I do on my birthday
If I get a whole lot more?

The ship sailed across the ocean
On its journey to Samarkand.
Would it reach the harbour safely
In that far and distant land?
Then the storm clouds began to gather
And the waves grew high and wide.
The ship was in trouble and failing,
Then it sank neath that mighty tide.
It lay on the floor of the ocean,
A prey of the sea's mighty wrath,
Then along came a diver and rescued the ship
From the bottom of my bath.

They say Wee Willie Winkie
Went rushing through the night
With nothing but a night-gown on –
He must have looked a sight.

There was a baby kangaroo
With very little else to do
But clamber up into his mother's pouch.

Mrs Kangaroo cried 'Ouch'
Because, of course, it must be told,
Although she loved her baby
His feet were very cold.

The warthog is a vulgar sort of animal,
It grunts and snorts and snuffles in the ground.
It's not the sort of animal to cuddle
And the nicest people don't want one around.

A teddy bear is soft and warm,
You can cuddle him in bed.
A puppy dog is cute and likes
To be stroked upon his head.
A kitten has fur as soft as silk
And a gerbil is just as fine.
I love my pet, but I don't know yet
How to cuddle my porcupine.

The walrus is not pretty,
He would make an awkward pet.
If you took him to bed to cuddle
Your pyjamas would get wet.

I hear a buzzing in the gloom,
A fly is flitting round my room.
It buzzes loudly round my head,
Just one quick swipe, I have it . . . dead.

I wonder sometimes what it is
That makes me love it so.
It hasn't really got a shape,
It's sort of 'so and so'.
It's brown with yellow patches,
It's not a teddy bear,
It isn't really anything
That you'd find anywhere.
It's not a kind of elephant,
It hasn't got a trunk,
It isn't stripy black and white,
It cannot be a skunk.
It has a leg and just one eye
In a battered sort of face,
I think it's just the sort of thing
To come from outer space.
It sleeps in bed beside me –
Never, never on the shelf.
I love it so, because you know
I made it all myself.

Shining star, shining bright,
I wish you could,
I wish you might,
Make my wish come true tonight.